THE COMPLETE CHILD

HOW TO PREPARE YOUR CHILD FOR ADULTHOOD

ANTHONY EKANEM

Dedicated to my family and the readers.

Contents

Foreword

Your child might be currently suffering from low levels of self-worth and self-confidence, but it does not have to be that way forever. You as a parent must take the necessary steps that will ensure that your child has a bright future full of potential and opportunities. The first place to start with this is to make sure your child feels good about themselves and has healthy levels of self-worth and self-confidence because these are two traits that make life's challenges bearable and possible of overcoming.

Without the building block of confidence, your child will likely be lost once it comes time for them to experience the real world. Without the capability of approaching unfamiliar people or taking on new tasks, the simplest tasks in life can be made a hundred times more difficult. Confidence is more than just an admired trait. To be truly successful in life and to be happy with themselves, your child must learn to be confident.

While motivating your child to build their self-confidence, remember the tips and tricks as well as the advice you have received from this book as it will be a valuable guide to assist you through the process. As well, make sure to keep in mind the negative outcomes that can become reality if your child doesn't have a healthy level of confidence.

Acknowledgements

I acknowledge all who inspired the writing of this book.

Choosing Your Child's School

CHAPTER ONE

Schooling Basics

Some schools are known for their academic excellence while others may be noted for their excellent sporting programmes. As a parent, you would have to decide which would be more suitable for your needs and that of the child in question.

If this decision proves to be a challenge at this stage, then finding a school that is competent in both areas would be acceptable. Convenience would also usually be another point to look into as no parent wants their child to have to sit through a one-hour ride just to get to school and another one-hour ride to get home.

This is also important from an emergency angle where the parent would be able to reach the child's school within the shortest time possible. Taking the time to check up on the school by speaking to others who have children already attending the facility would also be another way to gauge the suitability of the school. There is also the need to check the requirements, if any, that need to be met to be successfully admitted to the school.

What Are Your Child's Needs?

Finding out as much as possible about the schools within a suitable radius to fit the convenience of both child and parent would be a good start to choosing a school for the child. This should then be followed with more in-depth research as to what the schools identified can offer and how these will benefit the child in question.

There are several things to consider when it comes to the future of the child at the eventual choice made and the following are just some areas that should ideally be covered. Perhaps the first would be to contact the local educational centres to find out about all the various schools within the ideal perimeter to suit the initial need to limit the distance between the school and the place of residence of the family.

Once the school has been identified, then the parent would have to make a more in-depth study as to the suitability and comforts it can provide for the child who is going to be enrolled. Some children may need special attention for various reasons, and the school chosen should be able to cater for these needs adequately. The physical and mental comfort of the child at the school should ideally be an important factor when choosing the ideal school.

The services extended outside the actual study curriculum such as outdoor activities would also have to be considered if the child is particularly fond of the outdoors. Some children need to have this kind of learning experience to ensure they are kept interested and stimulated on the idea of education.

Considering if the child will eventually be comfortable with the other children attending the school is also another element to be considered. Some children are simply not able to adjust well to other cultures and styles that are foreign to them.

Think About Your Educational Values

Almost everyone has some idea of the educational values they would like to see their children adopt. Researching the type of values, the intended school follows would help to decide its suitability for both the parent and child.

The parent would have to first understand the value system they would like their children to be exposed to and then seek out the school using such a system. The values of education can be connected to either the actual teachings at the school or to the methodology used for the imparting of knowledge to the children at the school.

Both these are very different value systems that should ideally be understood before the decision to enroll is made. Here, the way and form the teachers impart the relevant curriculum outlines and content to the children would sometimes be a more important issue for the parent rather than what is being taught. This is mainly because most of the educational materials would already be dictated by the governing educational body at the time, thus the concerns in that area would not be as pivotal to the parent decision in terms of enrolment.

The method chosen by the school and the teaching staff would certainly be of some concern for the parent as they would want the child to have a good learning experience throughout the tenure at the school. Then there is the actual content that is being imparted in the form of education for the child eventually earmarked to attend the school chosen. For some parents, the content of the material to be taught would have to be in line with their belief systems thus creating an ideal extension of what the child is already taught at home.

CHAPTER TWO

Research the School Philosophy

Since the children will probably be in the school chosen throughout the tenure or phase of a particular period of educational needs, there should be some understanding of the school's philosophy and if it is suitable for both the child's needs and the parent's approval.

The school's philosophy should ideally be along the lines that would be approved by the parents intending to choose that school simply based on its perceived and touted philosophy elements. Besides the long-term effect, it will have on the child attending the school, other connective tissues would have to be considered, such as the overall costs, and eventually, the results the child is expected to be able to achieve with the school's help.

Ideally, the school's philosophy should be an extension of the family's value system as this will make it easier and less confusing for the child attending the school. Ensuring the school follows closely all the various ideas it advertised to the potential parent making enquiries, is very important as in some cases the parent eventually note that the school chosen for its philosophies does not follow what it initially promised.

Areas such as how the rules are enforced, what rules the school outlines, how the teaching staff tackles problems and problematic students, how the student are expected to simulate into the school environment, how the school encourages different cultures and beliefs into their system and many other equally important elements that will eventually impact the child's thought process in some way.

All the various philosophies can be explored by visiting the school in person and with the child or simply by talking to other families whose children attend the intended school of choice.

Research Extra Curricula and Programmes

Having complete overall schooling or education experience is very important for the eventual growth of the child both mentally and physically. Unfortunately for some, there is a growing trend to focus mainly on the educational needs of the child rather than the overall physical needs as well.

A healthy learning environment should also be able to encourage a good amount of physical activity to ensure the body and brain is adequately stimulated and alert to better cope with the educational materials the child is going to be expected to absorb. Therefore, it would be prudent to make the necessary inquiries as to the types of extra-curricular activities and programmes that are actively offered at the school.

This will also help the parent avoid the need to source for such complimenting activities outside the school system. This would not only be very inconvenient but would also incur more cost and time for the parent.

For the child too, it would be rather inconvenient to seek such added elements elsewhere and, in most cases, people will eventually opt not to focus on these areas and thus lose out in the long run to activities that could have proven to be useful in one way or another.

Having the choice of a good number of extra-curricular activities and varied programmes will also give the child the opportunity to be exposed to other interesting beneficial elements other than just plain education. This is also important as this is often the best way to spot talent in a particular field that is not particularly educationally based.

CHAPTER THREE

Visit the School

When the child is reaching school-going age, it would be the duty of the parent to start looking around for a suitable school for the child to attend. This should be done in a systematic manner that will ensure the most suitable and ideal educational environment is provided based on the choice made.

Part of the exercise of looking for a suitable school would be to talk to other parents whose children are attending the school intended, to get the views on the capabilities and other aspects of the school. This is important as it will give the parent an actual account of the school and its background as opposed to simply reading about the school in published material.

A lot of materials written on the school and its capabilities are usually written from an advertising and promotional style thus leaving a lot of elements glazed over to appear attractive to the prospective parent. After gaining as much information as possible on the school and deciding that it would probably be a good fit for the child, the next step would be to visit the school.

This will help the parent get a better feel for what is being offered and how the child will adapt to the new environment. It will also allow the parent to have a firsthand view of how things are done at the school.

Most schools especially the private ones will certainly go the extra mile to make the parent feel welcomed and will promote the school as best as they can so that a good impression is made. Those intending to visit a public school of their choice would also be able to do so without too much of a hassle.

If the Child is in the Wrong School

Most parents would ideally want their children to go to the best schools where the teaching and learning style is very competitive and good results are evident all year round. However, the parent should also know it is very important to choose a school that would most suit the individual child's needs and characteristics. This would be pivotal to the eventual complete rounded growth of the child both mentally and socially.

When a child is put into a school environment that is not suited to his or her capabilities, there could be some very detrimental effects that will eventually result in the child beginning to hate anything to do with education.

There are also a lot of cases where the child is very afraid to go to school, and this is usually caused by a variety of reasons, which range from an uninteresting curriculum to inadequate teaching tools. There is also the possibility of not wanting to go to school because of bullying issues that are prevalent and not taken seriously by the school authorities thus causing a lot of problems for the physically weaker students.

Academically, if the child does not feel stimulated by the programmes offered at the school, there would be the danger of boredom seeping in, and this too could create problems as the child seeks fulfilment elsewhere. This is most cases is of the negative kind, thus the importance of picking the right school for the child's future wellbeing.

Consider Your Finances

Providing a child with a good education will allow for the child to have a good foundation that will lead to better prospects in life. With the emergence and popularity of the private sector going into providing education, more people are choosing to opt for this style of providing education for their children.

Choosing between the two styles of public and private schooling should not be done lightly as this is a long-term commitment and would ideally require some serious thought. Deciding on the private schooling style can be very costly especially when a parent's earnings are no longer a guaranteed surety. This will eventually affect the child's progress and growth in many ways should the initial option of private schooling would now have to be changed to public schooling due to the lack of funds.

It is sometimes very difficult for the child to adjust both mentally and academically as most private education styles are said to be more competitive and well-rounded in the curriculum content and execution. In the private schooling style, there is also a lot more attention given to the individual child's needs which are not forthcoming in the public school system.

This is mainly because there are a lot more children squeezed into one classroom environment, thus leaving the teacher little choice but to focus on those who are interested in learning. Therefore, a child who is playful, inattentive, or simply too lazy to focus on what is being taught, will simply be left behind.

However, if the focus is on providing the child with a good education, the parents should explore all types of private institutions and carefully work out the long-term

costs it would involve educating the child in such a
scenario.

How to Keep Your Child Healthy

CHAPTER FOUR

Keep Your Child Free from Disease

It's perfectly natural for parents to worry about their children getting sick. Of course, as a mother or father, you take responsibility for this aspect of your child's health. Here are some of the most important things you can do to protect your children from diseases:

Get Your Child Immunised

Vaccines are a hot topic these days. But the truth of the matter is that anti-vaccine groups are in the wrong. There are simply too many myths about vaccines being spread by misinformed people or by people who stand to profit because they sell alternative medicines, books, or health programmes.

In other words, believing that vaccines are bad is just as erroneous a belief as believing that Elvis Presley is still alive or that space aliens are living among us. The problem with the anti-vaccine belief is that it puts your children, and other children, at risk. So, get your children immunized, and follow the vaccination schedule recommended by their doctor. The World Health Organization regards vaccines as one of the most effective public health interventions, as it prevents about 2.5 million deaths among children every year. The CDC considers vaccination the 20th century's greatest achievement in public health.

Have Regular Visits to the Doctor

This starts early in the life of your child, and it shouldn't stop even as they are in their teens. According to the American Academy of Paediatrics, during your child's first three years there should be nine check-ups at least.

As they grow older, these visits to the doctor need to continue. Of course, some kids may not be all too happy with the idea, so be prepared to set your mind at ease. Kids worry about the pain, the manner of the doctor, or being separated from them. Sometimes it's just the fear of the unknown. You'll need to assuage your kid's feelings of anxiety, although it helps if you choose a kid-friendly clinic where the doctors are experienced or at least skilled in dealing with children. You may not want someone who acts like Dr House in that popular TV show from a few years ago.

You can also reassure your children that all healthy kids get regular check-ups. If your child is sick, you can support them by telling them gently about how the sickness isn't their fault and that the doctor can help.

Get Health Insurance

Nowadays, getting health insurance is a legal matter now. In most cases, you'll be forced to pay a fine if you don't have your kids insured. But it is also a practical matter. Without adequate health insurance, you may have to foot the medical bills yourself if your child gets sick. That will be far more costly than paying for insurance.

You can start by going to the comprehensive health care website so you can get Medicare or shop for an insurance plan. These three things cover the very basics of protecting your children from disease. It starts with prevention using immunization, and then with regular visits to the doctor, you can monitor your child's health continuously. With health insurance, you have the means to make sure that your children get the care and medical treatment they require.

Feed Them Well

Introduce Them to Exercises

There was a time when quite a few parents were too concerned about their overly active children, which many believe had given rise to a lot of misdiagnoses of ADHD (attention deficit hyperactivity disorder). But nowadays parents are worrying about inactivity, especially with the popularity of console games, smartphone and tablet video games, the Internet, and of course huge LCD TVs.

Limiting Inactive Entertainment

This is probably the first order of business for many parents whose kids stay glued to the TV screen or computer monitor. Limiting a child's exposure to these things can get difficult as kids get older, so it's better if you start early.

The first thing you need to teach children is that watching TV and playing video games are *privileges* that you allow them and not something they are entitled to. So that means you can forbid TVs in kids' bedrooms, disallow TV watching during meals and while doing homework, or even disallow them during weekdays.

The Internet is a different matter, however, because children do need to use them especially for doing their homework. Your best bet is to make sure that your PC is in the living room so that you can monitor their Internet use so you can see that they're not viewing inappropriate content.

Encouraging Exercise

The next step is getting your kids to get off the couch or bed and to become more active. That's not too hard. All you need to do is to *find out* just what kind of activities your kids enjoy. So, for younger children, you can have them play simple tag games, skating, playing with a ball, riding a horse, riding a bike, or flying a kite. Many of these things can be taught to kids, such as ball games and riding a bike. You can teach them yourself or arrange for someone knowledgeable to teach them.

You can also support their desire to play sports. Lots of sports such as baseball have versions for kids. Just don't go overboard and *force* your children to learn. This may cause your kid to rebel and refuse to play anymore. Becoming an overbearing parent who forces their children to excel in sports is not only unbecoming but also counterproductive if your goal is to keep your children healthy through physical activity.

Safety Precautions

Of course, getting injuries is going to be part of the deal when you have an active child. This is going to be unavoidable, unfortunately. But you can limit the severity of the injuries by making sure that your children are adequately protected. Many activities and sports mandate that children wear helmets and protective gear. Make sure your child wears them when engaged in sports.

You should also always have a first aid kit ready in your car and home. And finally, don't forget to teach your children some rudimentary first aid measures as well.

CHAPTER SEVEN

Protect Them from Household Accidents

You may have heard that accidents are the leading cause of death in children. While that's a rather harrowing statistic, at least many of these accidents are preventable. That means you'll need to keep your home (and your car) safe for your kids. If you have a baby, then your first task is to make sure you get a safe crib. Check that the crib model hasn't been recalled for safety reasons. You should also make sure that it has been assembled correctly.

Proofing the Home for Younger Children

For toddlers and pre-schoolers, you'll need to remember that they can be very active, and they can crawl just about anywhere. So that means you need to keep cabinets locked, dangerous stairs blocked, and the pool well-fenced. Make sure there are no dangerous sharp edges and corners on which a child can hit their head.

You'll also need to remember that young children like to put things in their mouths. So, this means locking up toxic materials high up where young children can't find them. Other small items which may present a choking hazard must also be collected and kept out of reach.

This may not be enough though, so for very young children constant supervision may be required. In cars, special seats for younger children should be a priority.

Protecting Older Children

Just because a child is already older, it doesn't mean they're automatically wiser. So, protect them from places and appliances which can hurt them especially when they're alone. Kitchen and ironing appliances are good examples. As children get older, they should be taught how to handle these things safely.

Some households have firearms. While some families advocate educating young children about firearm safety, it is still a good idea that children do not have access to firearms unless they are with a knowledgeable adult. At the very least, guns and rifles should be locked securely so that children couldn't use them when you're not there.

Alarms and Safety Procedures

One of the more concrete ways you can make your home safe is by getting the appropriate alarms, so you know when something is wrong. This means installing smoke alarms and carbon monoxide detectors. You may also want to install burglar alarms to supplement your locks.

Then of course you should have a first aid kit available. As an adult, you may want to learn CPR yourself. At the very least, you should have the appropriate emergency phone numbers listed on your mobile phone and near your landline. Aside from the usual 911, you need the number of the local fire department, emergency hospital, and poison control. Then as your children grow older, they should also learn the basic safety procedures. If you have a fire extinguisher, they should know when and how to use it. They should have a clear plan of action when various alarms (burglar, fire alarm, etc.) go off.

Something always goes wrong, and that's a fact of life. You can prevent many accidents from happening but preventing them all may not be feasible. Alarms tell you when these things happen, and safety plans and procedures help you know what to do when bad things happen.

CHAPTER EIGHT

Teach Them Good Habits

Many parents are always worried about their kids' safety even when they're all grown up. The good news is you can help protect your kids by teaching them some habits. We all know about filthy habits like smoking, taking drugs and drinking alcohol which we forbid our children to try. You probably also educate them about avoiding unhealthy habits like drinking soda and eating junk food all the time. But you can also teach them to adopt healthy habits too.

Hygienic Habits

Let's start with hygiene since it's a basic aspect of growing up. This means making sure your kids wash up every day, wash their hands before eating, change clothes daily, and refrain from using other people's glasses and utensils. But one habit that must be taught properly is oral hygiene. Children must learn to brush and floss their teeth properly. While many parents teach these habits, it's still unfortunate that many kids don't know how to brush and floss their teeth. So you need to teach them these things.

Safety Habits

These habits include checking both sides of the street before crossing and using a seatbelt. These things should be taught religiously so they become automatic for children even as they grow up. Then there are the habits that children need to learn when using dangerous tools, such as tools in the garage and appliances in the kitchen. All these things must be shown and practised regularly, and you need to be there when your kids get some hands-on experience.

This extends to healthy habits when driving. Aside from using seatbelts, your children should learn to ignore their phones when they're learning to drive. They should learn to ignore any sort of distraction. They need to learn to be wary of strangers who talk to them when you're not around. Even people they know can also be dangerous, such as drunken friends behind the wheel of a car. They should also develop the habit of avoiding dangerous items like knives and guns if you're not there with them to supervise them.

Healthy Nutritional Habits

One habit you can teach your kids is to incorporate vegetables into their diet. This is the most challenging aspect of teaching proper nutrition. Broccoli and spinach just don't taste as delicious as hotdogs, pizza, and ice cream.

But they can learn to include vegetables if they develop a habit of eating them when they're still young. You can do this by eating veggies with them and making it evident that you like the taste. It's like beer—kids drink them because they see the adults drink them even if the taste isn't exactly like soda. They can learn to view veggies the same way, by learning to enjoy them because you enjoy them too.

Remember, a habit is something you do without thinking, simply because it's the way you learned to do things. By getting a child used to eating veggies and fruits, at least you'll know they'll be healthy when they get older.

Create Confidence in Your Child

CHAPTER NINE

Confidence Basics

Confidence is extremely important for a child to develop in the early stages of their life. It is important because it is needed to overcome many obstacles that your child will face in life. It is the job of the parent of the child to help the child build self-confidence. There are many ways that you can help your child build confidence.

Building your child's self-confidence will not only make them feel good about themselves but also prepare them for the future as well. You may find yourself asking: What can I do to give my child higher self-confidence? The answer is not difficult and there are several things you can do daily that will help and they will only take a few minutes.

If you are new to parenting, there are probably many things that you are not completely sure of how to do. One of these things may be how important building confidence in your child is or how to build confidence. Do not worry; just as every other challenge you have faced in life, it is achievable. All you need to do is learn some helpful techniques and set aside some extra time for your child and building their self-confidence will be as easy as a walk in the park.

A person's confidence levels as an adult are greatly impacted by the level of confidence that they had as a child.

This is one of the main reasons why it is so important that you instill a healthy amount of confidence in your child. With a little bit of effort and time, your child will surely develop this crucial life skill.

There are a few things that as a parent you will need to do. The following are some examples:

Always Make Time

You must always make time for your child, no matter how busy you are! Showing that your child comes before everything else is an excellent way of building a child's self-confidence and self-worth. It is advisable to take the time to schedule activities with your child that can help with the process of building their confidence. This could be taking them to do something they are good at or maybe even taking them to try something new. This will show them that they are talented which is a great confidence booster. One example could be taking a child to the park for a game of ball. If your child is not into sports, take them to an event that will allow them to show their knowledge on things and always be sure to show how impressed you are.

Don't Be Too Hard

Although it is important not to be too easy on your child, it is also important not to be too tough on your child as well. Being too easy on your child will likely not instill proper morals in a child or teach them to be responsible. On the other hand, being too tough will likely lead to low self-confidence because a child will feel as if they never do anything right. You as a parent must find the middle ground and be equal with your discipline. Not every child will respond to the same type of parenting, so it is important to experiment and see what works best when it comes to building your child's confidence.

Be a Positive Example

It is your job as a parent to set a positive example for your child and to be a role model. One of the personality traits that your child will likely learn from you is your level of self-confidence. You must always appear as if you have a situation under control and that you completely believe in yourself. Also, never talk negatively about yourself in front of your child because this will likely cause them to develop the same habit.

Watch Out for Bullies

Bullying is becoming increasingly more popular. This is likely stemming from the fact that kids can bully one another from any time and any place, thanks to social media. Bullying is probably one of the quickest ways a child's self-confidence can be destroyed. Bullies oftentimes suffer from low confidence in themselves. And to try to make themselves feel better, they try to lower others' confidence as well. This is why you must watch out for the signs of your child being bullied and put an immediate end to it! A few examples of behaviours your child may exhibit while being bullied are:

- Suddenly no longer wants to go to school
- Depression
- Anxiety
- Fear
- Less Social Interactions
- Not seeming Like Themselves
- Not Wanting to Talk About Their School Day

If you notice any of these signs you need to take immediate action!

CHAPTER TEN

Believe In Your Child

You must believe in your child. This is a very simple task to do and requires little effort. However, it is still very important. There are many ways that you can let your child know you believe in them. With enough effort and time, you will be able to find activities that greatly improve your child's confidence while showing that you believe in them.

Many people may be unsure of how to perform this step effectively and may not have an idea of where to begin. Are you one of these people? If the answer is yes, do not worry, children do not come with guidebooks, but you can get advice from places such as this book.

Show That You Believe in Them

The process of showing your child that you believe in them can be completed in many ways. Oftentimes, what works for one child may not have the same impact on another. This means that you will likely have to try different things until you find something that works. If you do not know where to start, a few examples are provided below:

Encourage Your Child to Try New Things

Encouraging your child to try new things is an excellent way of building their confidence and showing them that you fully believe in their abilities to accomplish something.

Pay attention to the things that your child tells you, especially when it comes to what they would like to do but do not feel that they would be any good at it. Use this situation to show you believe in them by encouraging them to try. Tell them that you believe in them and that they can do anything they set their mind to. It is important to explain to them that they may not be great at something when they first start but over time and with practice, they will get much better.

Push Them Out of Their Comfort Zone

When a child is stuck in a comfort zone, their chances of building their self-confidence are much slimmer than that of a child who is always challenging themselves. Teaching your child to challenge themselves will greatly improve their self-confidence while at the same time showing them that you believe that they can do anything.

Brag about Your Child

Bragging about your child can be a great way to build their confidence and show them that you believe in them. This is especially true if the bragging is done in front of them. Tell other people of their accomplishments and the things you think they will achieve in future as this will surely boost their confidence. Do not brag too much though because this may cause the child to become big-headed.

Achievements and Fears

Acknowledging your child's fears, as well as their achievements, is vital in the role of helping your child develop a healthy level of self-confidence. This is especially true when a child triumphs over their fear to accomplish something. It is important to remember that while trying to build a child's confidence, every little accomplishment should be noted. No matter how small the task is, your child will greatly benefit from your acknowledging their accomplishment.

The following paragraphs will give you some helpful information that can assist you with acknowledging your child's achievements and fears. It will serve as your guide so pay careful attention and make sure to retain all the information as it will surely help your child in becoming a self-confident person.

Praise Their Achievements, Understand Their Fears

A parent's role of praising their child's achievements as well as understanding their fears are two topics that we will go over in this chapter. A parent needs to understand that both are equally important when it comes to the process of instilling confidence in their child.

We will go over the importance of and the ways to praise a child's achievements first.

Praise Their Achievements

Praising your child's achievements, no matter how small they may seem to you, is vital in the process of creating confidence. This will make your child feel good about themselves and will also create self-confidence because they will feel as if they are constantly doing things that impress you.

Praising your child's achievements can have more of a positive outcome than constantly pointing out the negative things your child might do. This is not surprising since always pointing out the wrong thing a child does make them feel as if they cannot do anything right. On the other hand, always praising your child's achievements and not talking to them about mistakes that they are making will have negative outcomes as well. This is because the child will feel as if they can do nothing wrong. It is important to find a healthy balance between pointing out mistakes and praising achievements.

When praising your child's achievements, you must be careful to spoil or over-treat them. If you provide your child with a large reward every time they complete a small task, they will naturally begin to think that this will happen every time they do something. This can lead to negative behaviours when the rewards stop as the child will be confused about why they no longer receive a reward for a certain task. It is advised that rewards be saved for bigger accomplishments. When it comes to smaller achievements, verbal recognition or a pat on the back will suffice just fine.

Understand Your Child's Fears

Understanding your child's fears also play a big role in the development of your child's self-confidence. You may be asking: "How can fear make my child more confident in himself?" The answer is the fact that overcoming fear can boost a person's self-confidence dramatically. While trying to overcome fears, it is important that you first understand them.

You do not want to set your child up for failure. Some of the things they may be scared to attempt may be too difficult for them. One of the worst things you can do while trying to build a child's confidence is put them in a situation where they will not win. You need to talk to your child and discover what it is that they are afraid of attempting and determine if it would be a good idea to push your child toward facing those fears.

Once you understand your child's fears and have determined the possible negative and positive outcomes of facing them, you may decide to motivate your child to face those fears. Accomplishing a task that a child once feared would fail is probably one of the best ways to build self-confidence. This is because this process shows them that they can do things, no matter how hard they are or scared they were if they just put their mind to it.

It is important to not push your child into facing too many of their fears. Pushing your child too hard may result in an outcome completely different from the one you desire. It may make the child anxious which could have an impact on the rest of their life. This makes further lower their self-confidence because the anxiety may keep them from being able to accomplish other tasks that they could do effortlessly at one point.

CHAPTER ELEVEN

Teach Them to Learn from Their Mistakes

There is no perfect person in the world. Everyone makes mistakes. The important thing is that we learn to develop ourselves and learn lessons from our mistakes. We must then use these lessons to keep us from making future mistakes of a similar type. It is all part of the growing process. It is the same for a child who needs to build self-confidence.

Help Them Learn

Your child has been in the world much less time than you have. Therefore, it only makes sense that the responsibility of teaching your child how to learn from mistakes fall upon you. As a parent, you have surely had to do these many times in the past and have much more experience with it than your child. As stated before, everyone makes mistakes, and no one is perfect. What divides people into those who succeed and those who don't is whether a person learns from their mistakes or not.

Building your child's self-confidence is possible through success, and success is possible through your child learning from their mistakes. You must teach your child not to be too hard on themselves or beat themselves up when they make a mistake. You must teach them to look at the situation from a logical standpoint and determine the things that they could have done differently to get a more desirable outcome. You will be surprised at how much this will boost your child's self-confidence. This process will mature your child's thinking process and they will be more confident because they will know that even if they fail at something the first time, they will determine their mistakes, try again, and succeed.

Not teaching your child about learning from their mistakes will eventually have negative outcomes on your child's self-confidence. If your child does not learn from their mistakes, they will likely keep making the same mistakes. This can make a child feel as if they are stuck in a rut or like success is hopeless. They will feel like they cannot do anything and their motivation toward life will slowly spiral downward. A perfect example of this would be most people in correctional institutions, whether adult or juvenile.

If you ask most of the people in there, they will likely say that they never had anyone teach them the value of learning from their mistakes. These people continued to make the same mistakes until they felt as if life was hopeless and completely gave up on trying to be successful. You do not want this to happen to your child. For you to avoid a situation like this, you must teach your child the importance of learning from their mistakes.

Accept Who Your Child Is

Accepting a child for who they are is usually not a difficult task for a parent to perform. On the other hand, there are instances where certain things about a child bother their parents. This can be extremely damaging to a child's self-confidence because their parents are supposed to be a source of continued approval and affection. There are certain things that a child may not be able to change about themselves and you will have to accept them if you ever want your child to be happy and have high levels of self-confidence.

The following paragraphs will provide you with some examples of the types of things some parents may have to learn to accept. Keep in mind, some of these things may be difficult to accept or may even go against your religious background, but if you want your child to be confident and succeed you must accept them.

Accept Your Child for Who They Are

There may be certain things about your child that you wish could be different. The truth is, your child cannot change certain things about themselves. You cannot blame your child for who they are, they did not ask to be brought into the world, you decided to give them life. Your child may also do certain things in their life that you do not approve of, but you must accept them as reality and figure out a way to help your child change the behaviours.

The following are some examples of types of things your child cannot change about themselves.

Sexuality

This is probably the area where most parents have a hard time accepting their children for who they are. This may be due to moral standpoints, or it may be due to religious backgrounds and personal beliefs. No matter what the reason is, you must learn to accept your child for who they are. Showing your child that you love them for who they are will greatly improve their self-confidence and make them feel much better about themselves. Apart from this, trying to force your child to change something about themselves such as sexuality will cause many difficulties for a child in life. They will most likely become confused about who they truly are, and this will surely destroy their future and confidence.

Likes and Dislikes

You must learn to accept your child's likes, dislikes, and interests. You must understand that just because you want your son to grow up to be a football player or your daughter to be a beauty queen does not mean they want the same for their life. You need to encourage your child to do the things they like in life, even if they do not adhere to your set dreams and goals of your child. After all, it is their life, and they are the ones who must live it; parents are just passengers on the journey used as guidance.

Accept Your Child's Strengths and Weaknesses

It is important for you as a parent to understand that it may not be possible for your child to live up to all your expectations. You must remember to be realistic with your expectations for your child and to be understanding when they cannot live up to one of them. If you constantly show disapproval when a child cannot meet one of your expectations, you will destroy the child's confidence and make them feel like a lesser person or worthless. Showing your child that you will accept them if they try their best in everything, they do will surely boost their confidence and make them happier people with a more successful life.

These were just a few examples of the countless things you may have to accept about your child one day. As stated before, you do not have to like everything your child does, but you must learn how to accept it, not only for the confidence and well-being of the child but also for your own as well.

CHAPTER TWELVE

Take Interest in Your Child's Life

While your child is growing, you need to be actively involved in their lives and provide opportunities for growth if you want them to be full of confidence and be successful. Spending time with your child is all that this step requires. Do some activities with your child that they enjoy and use this time to learn more about your child's life. The more you know about what is going on in your child's life the better you will be able to help them in building their confidence.

Here are some helpful hints for being involved in your child's life and opening opportunities for them.

Be Involved

It is important that as a parent you make sure to be involved in your child's life. This does not mean when it is convenient for you, it always means even when difficult. You may have to do things you are not interested in or attend events that you may find boring. It does not matter; you need to be involved. Being involved in your child's life shows them that you truly care for them and at the same time build their self-worth and self-confidence.

You need to ask your child questions about their life and about how they feel everything is going for them. You need to try to figure out the areas where you can help them to build their confidence and open new opportunities for them during these discussions. A great time to do this would be during dinner, with the family eating at the dining table and not in front of the TV on the couch.

While it is important to get out and do things that your child is interested in while trying to be more involved with their life, you need to set specific family times that the entire family spends time. This greatly nurtures the health of a family relationship and makes your child more likely to open to you about their life. If your child is open with you, they will tell you what is holding their confidence back which allows you to help them gain their confidence back and be successful.

You need to take extra care not to pry into your child's life too deeply. Trying to be too involved in your child's life might make your child feel as if you are invading their life or trying to control it. You must keep in mind that it is their life and although you may not agree with some of their decisions, you must let them learn on their own. Having a healthy amount of involvement without trying to invade your child's life is a perfect recipe for a happy family and a confident child.

Give Responsibilities

Responsibilities in life are very important for a child, especially when it comes to building their confidence. You must be realistic with the responsibilities you set for your child because you do not want to doom them to failure. Setting responsibilities that are too difficult may result in failure which will further lower your child's confidence. On the other hand, a child who performs their responsibilities correctly will be granted better self-confidence.

The following are some ideas on where to start when it comes to setting responsibilities for your child.

Set Responsibilities, Be Realistic

While setting responsibilities for your child, it is extremely important that you set realistic responsibilities. It is advised that you start with simple responsibilities and work up toward the larger ones, once the smaller ones can be executed with minimal effort. The ideal basic responsibilities to start with for children would be tasks such as cleaning their room and making their bed. After they can handle this daily, you may want to begin adding additional responsibilities such as doing the dishes a few times a week or vacuuming the carpet.

As a child gets older and can handle more responsibilities, it is time to take their responsibilities more difficult. One idea that may be suitable is getting your child a pet. Something smaller than a dog is advised because most people do not realize how much care a dog needs. It may be better to start with an animal such as a hamster or some fish. The act of having to feed this animal daily, while taking care of its other needs, will help your child to become more responsible. Properly completing their responsibilities will also create more self-confidence for them since they will see they can do challenging things.

Instilling responsibilities into your child's daily life will be a challenge at first, but with determination and effort, it will be effective in boosting your child's confidence.

Poor Self Confidence

A child with poor self-confidence will almost certainly have a much more challenging life than that of a confident child. Having good confidence causes a person to have certain traits in their character while having low self-confidence creates negative traits in people's characters.

The following are a few examples of the countless disadvantages that low confidence can have on your child's life.

The Dangers of Low Self-Confidence

Many different disadvantages come with having low confidence levels. These disadvantages can have a huge negative impact on a person's current life as well as their future. That is why it is so important to instill high levels of confidence in your child, even from a very early age.

Some examples of the negative impacts low self-confidence can have on a child are as follow:

Scared to Try New Things

If your child has low levels of self-confidence, they will likely find it difficult to try new things. The fear of failure will take them over, time and time again. This fear will stop them dead in their tracks every time they think of trying to do something new.

Bad Social Impacts

If your child suffers from low self-confidence, they will likely have trouble with their social life in the future. A task as simple as approaching someone to say hello can feel impossible if a person has low self-confidence.

To be able to speak to other people and keep your head high, you must have good self-confidence. This can also extend into the classroom and your child's learning. For example, if your child has very low levels of confidence, they will likely be afraid of approaching a teacher and asking for help with what they don't understand. They would rather just take the failing grade because they do not have to interact socially in this way.

Emotional Issues

Certain emotional problems will likely be caused by long periods of low confidence. These emotional problems may include loss of happiness, anxiety, depression, irritability, and in extreme cases, suicide. Suicide most often occurs when a child feels as if they are nothing and will never be anything. Sometimes they hide this feeling from their parents and other times their parents do not pay enough attention, either way, it is terrible that a child would do this. All these emotional issues can have impacts on your child's present and future life. That is why it should be your top priority as the parent of your child to ensure that they feel great about themselves and that they have high levels of self-confidence.

Just keep in mind all the negative consequences that were discussed in this chapter while remembering that there are countless more and you will surely be motivated to start helping your child to better their confidence.